Writing for *Challenger 1–4*
Teacher's Manual

McVey & Associates, Inc.

NEW READERS PRESS

1-56420-014-0

Copyright © 1994 New Readers Press
New Readers Press
Division of ProLiteracy Worldwide
1320 Jamesville Avenue, Syracuse, New York 13210
www.newreaderspress.com

Printed in the United States of America
9   8   7   6

All proceeds from the sale of New Readers Press materials
support literacy programs in the United States and worldwide.

CONTENTS

WRITING FOR CHALLENGER 1 SCOPE & SEQUENCE

Lesson	STRAND 1			STRAND 2	STRAND 3		STRAND 4	STRAND 5	STRAND 6		STRAND 7
	Fill in the Missing Word (1)	Add Another Word	Fill in the Missing Words (2)	Choose the Right Word	Answer the Questions (1-word change)	Answer the Questions (multiple change)	Unscramble the Sentences	Put These Sentences in Order	What Do You Think? (sentence completion)	Complete the Sentences	Personal Questions
1	X				X		X	X	X		
2	X				X		X	X	X		
3	X				X		X	X	X		
4					X		X	X	X		
5		X			X		X		X		X
6	X					X		X	X		X
7	X	X				X	X		X		X
8	X	X				X		X	X		
9	X			X		X	X		X		
10	X			X		X	X				X
11	X			X		X		X		X	
12	X			X		X		X	X		
13			X			X	X			X	
14			X	X		X		X	X		
15			X			X	X			X	
16			X			X		X	X		
17				X		X	X			X	
18				X		X	X	X	X		
19				X		X	X			X	
20			X			X	X	X	X		
Review	X						X	X	X	X	X

WRITING FOR CHALLENGER 2 SCOPE & SEQUENCE

Lesson	STRAND 2 Choose the Right Word	STRAND 4 Unscramble the Sentences	STRAND 5 Put These Sentences in Order	STRAND 6 What Do You Think? (sentence completion)	STRAND 6 What Do You Think? (questions w/ starters)	STRAND 6 What Do You Think? (questions w/o starters)	STRAND 7 Personal Questions	STRAND 8 Combine the Sentences (2 sentences)	STRAND 9 Use These Words in Sentences	STRAND 10 Complete These Paragraphs
1	X	X		X			X	X		
2	X	X		X			X	X		
3	X	X		X			X	X		
4	X	X		X			X	X		
5	X	X		X			X	X		
6				X			X	X	X	
7		X					X	X	X	
8	X		X	X			X			
9	X	X	X	X			X	X	X	
10	X	X		X			X			
11			X		X			X	X	X
12	X				X					X
13		X	X		X			X	X	X
14	X				X					X
15		X	X		X			X	X	X
16	X					X				X
17		X				X		X	X	X
18	X	X				X				X
19		X				X		X	X	X
20			X			X			X	X
Review		X	X			X		X		X

WRITING FOR CHALLENGER 3 SCOPE & SEQUENCE

Lesson	STRAND 5 Put These Sentences in Order	STRAND 6 What Do You Think? (sentence completion)	STRAND 6 What Do You Think? (questions w/ starters)	What Do You Think? (questions w/o starters)	STRAND 8 Combine the Sentences (2 sentences)	STRAND 8 Combine the Sentences (3 sentences)	STRAND 9 Use These Words in Sentences	STRAND 10 Complete These Paragraphs	STRAND 10 Write a Paragraph (guided)	STRAND 10 Write a Paragraph (open-ended)
1		X			X		X	X		
2	X	X					X	X		
3	X	X			X		X	X		
4	X		X				X	X		
5			X		X		X	X		
6	X		X				X	X		
7				X		X	X		X	
8	X			X			X		X	
9				X		X	X		X	
10	X			X			X		X	
11				X		X	X		X	
12	X			X			X		X	
13				X		X	X		X	
14	X			X			X		X	
15				X		X	X		X	
16	X			X		X	X			X
17				X			X			X
18				X		X	X			X
19	X			X			X			X
20				X		X	X			X
Review	X			X		X				X

WRITING FOR CHALLENGER 4 SCOPE & SEQUENCE

Lesson	STRAND 5 Put These Sentences in Order	STRAND 6 What Do You Think? (questions w/o starters)	STRAND 7 Combine the Sentences (3 sentences)	STRAND 8 Combine the Sentences (4 sentences)	STRAND 9 Use These Words in Sentences	STRAND 10 Write a Paragraph (open-ended)	Write a 3-Paragraph Summary (guided)	Write Paragraphs (3 guided paragraphs)	Write Paragraphs (3 open-ended paragraphs)
1	X	X			X	X			
2		X	X		X	X			
3	X	X			X	X			
4		X	X		X	X			
5	X	X			X	X			
6		X		X	X	X			
7	X	X			X		X		
8		X		X	X		X		
9	X	X		X	X			X	
10		X			X		X		
11	X	X		X	X		X		
12		X		X	X		X		
13	X	X			X			X	
14		X		X	X				X
15	X	X			X				X
16		X		X	X				X
17	X	X			X				X
18		X		X	X				X
19	X	X		X	X				X
20		X		X	X				X
Review		X				X		X	

Chapter 1

Introduction to Writing for Challenger 1–4

The four *Writing for Challenger* books have been developed to provide additional writing practice for learners who are using the first four *Challenger Adult Reading Series* books. Educators generally recognize that reading and writing reinforce each other and that writing skills should be developed simultaneously with reading skills. This manual describes the types of exercises in the writing books, discusses reasons for integrating writing instruction and practice into reading lessons, and suggests ways to do so.

Systematic Writing Skills Development

Writing for Challenger is designed to develop systematically the skills necessary for writing sentences, paragraphs, and three-paragraph essays. Exercise formats become familiar while increasing in difficulty and sophistication. Related strands of exercises also become progressively more difficult. These strands include filling in missing words, unscrambling sentences, putting sentences in order, combining sentences, completing sentences and paragraphs, and writing guided and open-ended paragraphs. Each type of exercise becomes gradually more challenging as learners progress through the books.

Thinking Skills Development and Reinforcement

The exercises in the writing books develop and reinforce thinking skills as well as writing skills. For example, when sentences that are listed in a random order are put into a logical time order, sequencing skills are developed. Exercises that ask for reasons why an incident in a story may have taken place reinforce concepts of cause and effect. Learners develop basic skills in logic and reasoning as they write coherent sentence and paragraph responses to questions.

Reading Skills Reinforcement

The lessons in the *Writing for Challenger* books are closely tied to the corresponding lessons in Books 1–4 of the *Challenger* reading series. The content and vocabulary in each writing lesson is directly related to that in the lesson in the corresponding reading book. Comprehension of the reading selections is aided by doing exercises in the writing books that ask students to write about personal opinions and experiences related to the readings. Thus, reading comprehension and vocabulary building are reinforced while writing and thinking skills are being developed.

Because *Challenger* is a controlled-vocabulary reading series, the vocabulary in the writing books is also controlled. Except for a very few words in Book 1, the words used in the writing books are those that have been introduced in the corresponding reading books.

How Writing for Challenger Is Organized

Each book contains from nine to eleven types of exercises. Four or five of these exercise types are selected for each two-page lesson. The exercises are designed to develop writing, thinking, and composing skills. Exercise formats are used repeatedly so learners recognize how to do them even though the tasks involved become increasingly more difficult. Many exercises carry over from one level to the next, thus providing continuity between books as well as within books.

Strands of exercises develop specific writing skills. In some instances, a single type of exercise constitutes a strand, but in others, two or three related exercises comprise a strand. The exercises in each strand become progressively more challenging. For example, the sentence-combining exercises begin with two sentences being combined into one. Later, students are asked to combine three and then four sentences into a single one.

In another strand, sentence completion exercises lead to paragraph-completion exercises. Following these are guided and then open-ended one-paragraph compositions. Finally, both guided and open-ended three-paragraph compositions appear. The scope and sequence charts on pages 4–7 show the relationships among exercises. The various exercise formats and their relationships to each other are discussed in Chapter 2, "Suggestions for Teaching the Exercise Strands."

Involving the Adult Learner

Adults bring to any learning situation a wealth of experience and knowledge. They bring personal needs and goals, too. It is important that the adult learners' existing knowledge and experience be recognized, used, and valued. It is also extremely important that learners' needs and goals be the focus of instruction.

In the very first sessions with your adult learners, you can set the tone by involving them in discussions about their interests, what they hope to gain from the instruction, and what they need to learn in order to use reading and writing in their everyday lives. You can use the information you gain to tailor their reading and writing practice to their goals and interests. As you demonstrate your willingness to respond to their needs, they can come to feel more in control of their own learning. This in turn will lead them to feel an increased sense of ownership in the process. When you collaborate with your adult learners in choosing the subject matter and types of writing for them to practice, you validate their knowledge, skill, and experience. In addition, they will gain more from the practice because it is more meaningful to them.

You can gain insights into learners' needs and goals through their writing, as well. Many exercises in the writing books are designed to give students opportunities to express their opinions, draw from their personal experiences, and tell what interests them. Responses to these questions can help you to plan additional activities of interest to learners. As students gain confidence in their writing abilities, their writing opportunities can broaden to include writing that they need to do for their homes or jobs—reports, letters, or notes to their children's teachers, for example. Chapter 3, "Teaching Writing," and Chapter 4, "Developing Skill in the Writing Process," discuss some of the issues involved and techniques to use in helping adults to improve their writing skills.

Chapter 2

Suggestions for Teaching the Exercise Strands

Every exercise in *Writing for Challenger* is tied in some way to the corresponding lesson in the reading book, with most exercises expanding on or reinforcing the reading selection. For example, some exercises require the manipulation of vocabulary or sentences from the reading, while others call for responses that are based on events or concepts in the reading. In some exercises, learners may be asked to write about their personal experience with or opinion about something that took place in the reading. In many exercises, students have the opportunity to answer comprehension questions or to write a brief summary of the reading.

In addition to reading-related exercises, there are exercises that reinforce vocabulary, grammar, or technical aspects of writing by providing practice with specific elements introduced in the reading lessons, such as adding endings or forming irregular past tenses of verbs.

The following section presents the exercise strands and tells what skills each strand is intended to develop. It also describes the exercise formats in each strand and gives suggestions for teaching students how to work with them.

Strand 1: Filling in Missing Words

Filling in Missing Words is an exercise strand that runs through Book 1. In this strand, learners select appropriate words from a list and write them in blanks to complete sentences. Although the exercises require very little actual writing, they do reinforce the reading lesson, require learners to use context clues, review sentence structures, and provide a type of exercise that most learners can complete successfully. Having exercises in Book 1 that learners can complete successfully helps them to overcome their fear of writing.

There are three exercise formats in this strand. "Fill in the Missing Word" and "Add Another Word" call for a single word to be chosen from a word list and added to a sentence. "Fill in the Missing Words" calls for a pair of words to be chosen to complete a sentence.

When introducing these exercises, you may want to work through the first exercise of each type with any students who are not sure about how to proceed.

Strand 2: Choosing the Right Word

A more sophisticated fill-in-the-blank exercise strand appears later in Book 1 and in Book 2. In "Choose the Right Word" exercises, students are to choose from a pair of similar words the one that completes a sentence correctly. These exercises are designed to provide practice using correct grammar and syntax as well as word discrimination. For example, to complete the sentence "Don't talk so _____," the choice is between *loud* and *loudly*. The choices for the sentence "You stepped on my _____ and it hurt" are *food* and *foot*.

Again, you may want to work with students as they encounter this exercise format the first time. Make note of recurring problems that any student may have and plan individual remediation.

Strand 3: Answering Questions

The exercises in the Answering Questions strand appear in Book 1. They take two forms. Early in the book, students must change only one word in each question in order to form an answer. For example, the question "Who was late for work?" can be answered by simply changing *Who* to *Bob:* "Bob was late for work." Students must provide a complete written sentence in response to a question, but the exercise is structured in a way that offers a high probability of success.

When introducing this exercise, remember that students can be overwhelmed by facing a question-and-answer format for the first time. You can help them overcome their fears by pointing out that only one word needs to be changed to provide an answer to the question.

This is a good exercise to use as a model for developing additional practice and reinforcement activities. The questions you develop can be based on subject matter that ranges from current events to mathematics. Students can respond orally as well as in writing, but in both instances, they should respond in complete sentences. Continue to reinforce these simple question-and-answer structures even after students begin working with more complex sentences. This will help them to master the form and increase their overall confidence with the question-and-answer format.

The multiple-change version of the "Answer the Questions" format appears later in Book 1. In these exercises, learners must make multiple word and/or word-position changes in order to form a correct response. For example, the question "When did Bob go to see Aunt Louise?" can be answered "Bob went to see Aunt Louise after work." These question-and-answer structures generally reinforce those practiced in the corresponding reading lessons.

Sentence structures in these multiple-change exercises may be more difficult for learners to master than those in the earlier exercises in the strand. Work with students until they are able to complete the exercises with relative ease. Frequent reinforcement of the specific sentence structures contained in each exercise may be needed. Be alert to any forms that cause problems for an individual or the group, and develop additional examples for practice.

Strand 4: Unscrambling Sentences

The Unscrambling Sentences strand occurs in Books 1 and 2. In "Unscramble the Sentences" exercises, all the words that make up a sentence are provided in random order, and learners must write a logical sentence using all of the words. The sentences are related to, and frequently taken from, the corresponding reading selection, thus reinforcing comprehension and vocabulary.

An exercise of this type can be introduced by putting the listed words on index cards. By manipulating the cards, students can experiment with different word combinations. When an acceptable sentence is formed, students can copy it on the lines provided.

"Unscramble the Sentences" exercises can be fun for many learners but can be extremely frustrating for people with certain types of learning disabilities. Watch for signs of frustration in students and, if necessary, give them the first three or four words of a sentence to get them started. If a learner is unable to complete the word-sequencing process successfully after a number of attempts with your help, you may wish to excuse the learner from this type of exercise altogether. Nothing is gained if people become so frustrated by one exercise that they won't try other types or, worse still, drop completely out of a learning situation.

Strand 5: Putting Sentences in Order

Putting Sentences in Order is an exercise strand that appears in all four books. Students are asked to determine the correct time order in which three to six randomly ordered sentences should appear and to copy the sentences in the correct order on blank lines. "Put These Sentences in Order" exercises provide sentence-copying practice without the tedium that often attends straight copying exercises. In order to avoid tedious recopying, however, have students number the sentences in the correct order and go over the numbering with them before they copy the sentences on the lines.

Since these exercises are usually based on the reading selection from the corresponding *Challenger* book, they help to reinforce vocabulary and comprehension while developing the critical thinking skill of sequencing.

You can use this exercise format to develop reinforcement exercises that review the details of current events or lessons from other classes, or that test comprehension of other reading materials. You can put sentences on the chalkboard and have students write them in the correct order for extra writing practice. You can also put the sentences on separate index cards and then have students put the cards in order and read them aloud for oral reading practice. For any exercises that you develop, remember that there should be only one logical order in which sentences can be placed. There may be times, however, when a learner puts the sentences in a sequence different from the one you had in mind. When this happens, accept any sequence that students can justify or explain and use the opportunity to discuss the different versions.

Strand 6: What Do You Think?

The What Do You Think? strand also appears in all four books. The exercise formats in the strand vary as the level of difficulty increases, but in most instances, the learner's personal experience, opinion, or point of view is sought. Students may be asked to reflect on events described in the corresponding reading selection or to respond with their own ideas to issues related to the reading.

In Book 1, the format used for this strand is a sentence-completion exercise. Sentence starters such as "Eddie lost his money because . . ." are provided, and students complete the sentences by telling what they think. In five lessons in Book 1, this strand is represented by "Complete the Sentences" exercises. In this variation, sentence starters such as "Dave lied to Joan when he said . . ." call for information from the reading selection rather than for the learner's personal opinion.

Midway through Book 2, the What Do You Think? strand evolves into a question-and-answer format. Questions are asked, and a sentence starter is given from which an answer can be formed. For example, the question

"Do you think your handwriting tells people about you?" is followed by the sentence starter "I think my handwriting . . ." The writing task involved is the same as for the earlier format with which students have become familiar. The addition of the question, however, prepares students for the final format in this exercise strand. In this variation, which begins late in Book 2, questions are asked, and students respond by writing complete sentences without the benefit of sentence starters.

You can use the exercises in this strand to develop readiness for teaching the writing process. Students can discuss their ideas for completing each sentence with you or with peers and then select the most appropriate response before actually writing. In this way, they can become accustomed to thinking before writing, which is the primary goal of prewriting activities in the writing process. (See Chapter 4, "Developing Skill in the Writing Process," for a thorough discussion of prewriting techniques.) Asking students to talk about possible responses will result in better sentences, and it will prepare them for more extensive prewriting activities later.

With this exercise strand, you can also introduce concepts related to revising. When learners have become comfortable with the exercise format, you can have them write two or more versions of their answers. Tell them to think of ways to say the same thing using slightly different words. Make sure they focus on trying to improve previous versions of the answer rather than on providing completely new forms of the answer. Using this technique, you can introduce students to the concept of revising without actually discussing it.

Strand 7: Personal Questions

The Personal Questions exercise strand occurs in Books 1 and 2. It gives learners the opportunity to answer questions of a general nature entirely in their own words. The questions, based on content covered in the corresponding reading lesson, allow more freedom of expression than many of the other exercises in the first two books. Learners who are capable of doing some free writing are usually stimulated by these opportunities, but even less-skilled students usually respond well to the challenge.

Prewriting techniques become important in doing these exercises. Have students talk about possible responses or, if students are ready, have them jot down their ideas in key words or phrases that they can use when writing their responses.

Strand 8: Combining Sentences

The Combining Sentences strand provides practice in manipulating words and sentences so students can understand complex sentence structures better and can develop variety and flexibility in writing. Students often need considerable practice combining short, choppy sentences into more complex sentence forms. "Combine the Sentences" exercises provide opportunities for students to combine sentences into a variety of more complex forms. Beginning in Book 2 with combining two sentences, this exercise strand increases in difficulty as three sentences and then four are combined in Books 3 and 4 respectively.

Students usually begin this type of exercise by simply combining the two given sentences into a compound sentence. You probably will need to help them go beyond compound sentences by providing clues such as "Try starting your sentence with *when*" or "Try using *because* in your sentence" when appropriate.

Suggested ways to combine the sentences are provided in the answer keys, but often there is more than one way to combine them. Encourage experimentation by accepting any combination that is reasonable. You can then discuss alternative combinations, comparing differences in emphasis, effectiveness, and meaning.

Sentence-combining skills can be reinforced with additional exercises you develop based on other lessons or on students' personal interests. Keep in mind the need to provide sentences that can be combined in a variety of ways.

Strand 9: Using Key Words in Sentences

The Using Key Words in Sentences strand begins in Book 2 and continues through Book 4. In "Use These Words in Sentences" exercises, students are given a list of key words taken from the corresponding reading selection. They are asked to write sentences about the reading selection using some of the listed words. There is no prescribed way to respond to this exercise. One person may choose to write three summary sentences, while another may recount unconnected incidents in the reading, and yet a third may express personal opinions about ideas in the reading.

For this type of exercise, students can do prewriting thinking on their own or with peers. Being generous with positive feedback about their responses will encourage them to experiment and to write freely. Nothing should be seen as being more or less important, better or worse. Work with students to make their writing stronger or clearer, but respect their choices of topic and form.

Strand 10: Writing Paragraphs

Paragraph writing is introduced midway through Book 2. This strand increases in difficulty through Books 3 and 4. In Book 2, "Complete These Paragraphs" provides two- or three-sentence paragraph starters. Students complete the unfinished sentences to develop paragraphs that reflect their personal opinions, points of view, experiences, or interests. This exercise format builds on the familiar sentence-completion format, so understanding how to do the exercise should not be difficult for learners.

Near the middle of Book 3, the strand evolves into "Write a Paragraph" exercises. The first format is a guided paragraph-writing exercise that provides a series of questions to answer. The questions appear in an unnumbered, stacked arrangement. A coherent paragraph can be developed by answering the questions in order and in complete sentences. As usual, the questions are related to the selection in the corresponding reading book lesson.

The paragraph-writing strand becomes increasingly more challenging as the guided writing format is replaced by an open-ended format, which appears late in Book 3 and continues in Book 4. In these more sophisticated exercises, starter questions are asked, but a coherent paragraph cannot be written solely by answering the questions. The writer must go beyond the specific questions to the implied questions or must supply supporting information or arguments. It is important, therefore, that students develop a good sense of what types of ideas can go together in a paragraph while they are practicing the guided writing version of the exercise.

This strand is further developed in Book 4 with "Write a Three-Paragraph Summary" and "Write Paragraphs." In both of these guided-writing exercise formats, students are asked to write three paragraphs rather than one. As in the guided single-paragraph format, questions are presented in a stacked arrangement, and answering them in complete sentences will result in coherent paragraphs. There is only one difference between "Write a Three-Paragraph Summary" and "Write Paragraphs": in the first, students are asked to summarize the reading, and in the second, students write about the reading rather than summarize it.

The final format of the strand appears in the middle of Book 4. These "Write Paragraphs" exercises are the culminating activities in the *Writing for Challenger* books. Open-ended questions are provided for writing three paragraphs related to the reading selection, and the student must determine the direction the writing takes. As in the open-ended single-paragraph format, a writer cannot develop coherent paragraphs solely by answering the questions. These exercises typically ask students to write their opinions or views about an issue or to support an idea with specific information.

Using the various paragraph-writing exercises as models, you can develop additional activities tailored to the interests of your students. Develop exercises to reinforce the increasingly sophisticated one- and three-paragraph exercises in this strand. Students will benefit from any additional activities that you develop. For instance, the more practice learners get with the guided format, the less trouble they will have with the open-ended format.

This exercise strand is particularly suitable for teaching and practicing the various steps in the writing process. Suggestions for doing this are included in Chapter 4, "Developing Skill in the Writing Process."

Chapter 3 ──────────────

Teaching Writing

As with any skill, people learn to write by writing. Particularly with adult students, the learning will progress more rapidly if their needs, interests, and goals dictate the kinds of writing they do and what they write about. This chapter gives suggestions on how to make writing a regular part of the *Challenger* reading program.

Providing Frequent Opportunities to Write

Adult students should begin writing at the same time that they begin reading instruction. Daily opportunities for writing result in the most rapid progress, even if the writing activity is very brief. Students usually make significantly greater gains by writing for 10 minutes every class session than if they write for 45 to 60 minutes once every two weeks. Extended writing opportunities are also important, but they are necessarily less frequent than shorter, more informal writing activities.

Many of the exercises in the *Writing for Challenger* books can be done in 10 or 15 minutes during class time. Exercises that require more thinking and writing can be done for homework. You can develop additional writing activities patterned after the exercises in the writing books based on current events and learners' interests.

These brief writing activities, however, won't accomplish all of the learners' writing goals. Opportunities for extended writing that can be more polished and formal also should be provided. Major writing activities can be integrated into your reading program by breaking them into individual steps and allowing enough time to do one step during class sessions each week. The steps in the writing process are discussed in Chapter 4.

Evaluating Student Writing

Working with adult students requires a great deal of flexibility and tailoring of instruction to individual needs. Instruction should begin at whatever skill level the individual student has reached, taking into account both problem areas and the skills already present. It is important not to waste a lot of time instructing students about things they already know. In order to determine what students know and what they need, you will have to evaluate the writing they do.

Adult students often think of evaluation as "getting a grade." For most student writing, you probably won't be giving grades. But it is important for you to look over all writing that students do in order to diagnose their problems and prescribe ways to overcome them. Otherwise, students will simply be reinforcing bad habits.

For many of the exercises in the writing books, it is appropriate to go over answers orally in class. This is particularly true for those that have a limited number of possible correct answers. However, taking additional time for you to look over exercises that call for individual responses, such as "What Do You Think?" and "Complete the Sentences," will give you valuable information about problem areas.

When looking over students' writing, you can make notes about individual strengths and weaknesses. You can also note any personal goals and interests that are revealed to guide you in making suggestions for topics to write about or discuss.

Remediating Writing Problems

Grammar, punctuation, spelling, capitalization, and other mechanics of writing often are taught in isolation. Basing instruction on problems discovered in actual student writing is more effective. It gives meaning and relevance to the lessons. After evaluating a student's writing, select one or two problems for the student to work on and provide instruction and reinforcement practice for those specific areas. Problems that occur repeatedly in the student's writing, such as leaving off an -ed ending from several verbs, often provide the most immediate improvement. You can also ask students what problem they would like to work on first. Adult students often know what skills they want to improve. The important thing to remember is to work on only one or two problems at a time. Keep lists of other difficulties for future remediation.

From the first lesson, students can begin to develop the habit of looking over their work after completing each writing exercise. This reinforces the concept that editing and proofreading are important steps in the writing process. Students often mistakenly believe that experienced writers produce polished pieces on the first draft.

For students who have very limited writing skills, beginning where they are can often mean encouraging them to use invented spellings. Adult students often are stymied when writing first drafts because they can't spell a word they want to use and they can't get beyond that point. Suggest that they put down the letters that they can hear in the word and draw blank lines for the parts that they don't know. For instance, a student wanting to write "an engine" in response to the sentence starter "I know how to fix . . ." in Lesson 2 of Book 1 might write n___jn. If none of the letters are known, the student can draw a blank for the whole word and go on to the rest of the sentence. When going over the exercise with the student, you can ask what the intended word is, write the word correctly, and have the student copy the word in the exercise book. For students with many spelling problems, it is a good idea to encourage them to keep personal spelling notebooks in which they can list alphabetically words that they use often and want to learn to spell.

Techniques for Teaching the Mechanics of Writing

Most problems with grammar, syntax, and the mechanics of writing that adult students have will be individual. Therefore, most instruction and remediation of these problems must be done on an individual basis. Whenever a problem is shared by a group, of course, instruction can be given to the group as a whole. But the greatest progress is made when a student feels a personal need to learn and the instruction is immediate. There are several strategies that can be used to personalize instruction and to make it immediate. Among them are using planned mini-lessons, spontaneous teaching opportunities, and the discovery approach to teaching.

Mini-lessons

Mini-lessons are short, focused segments of instruction within a class session. They are designed to deal with one discrete point of instruction.

They can be used with a single student or with a group, depending on whether the skill or concept being taught is needed by one or more students.

Mini-lessons can be designed to teach a point of grammar, correct use of punctuation, a spelling principle—almost any discrete skill a student needs to learn. When designing a mini-lesson for an individual student, plan to include only what can be taught in 5 or 10 minutes. If you are planning instruction for a group of students who share a problem, the mini-lesson could take 15 to 30 minutes to allow all students to respond at various points in the lesson.

It is usually best to plan a series of mini-lessons to deal with a specific problem. In the first lesson, you can introduce the point and provide instruction. Then one or more mini-lessons can provide practice and reinforcement.

Spontaneous Teaching Opportunities

Some of the best teaching and learning takes place when a learner asks a question or expresses an idea that opens a door to instruction. Unlike mini-lessons, teachable moments cannot be planned. However, your daily planning should provide enough flexibility for you to be able to take advantage of sudden teaching opportunities as they arise in a class session. For example, when a student recognizes that he has written a very long sentence and asks how he can fix it, you can seize that opportunity to teach him how to recognize complete thoughts and to break up run-on sentences.

Sudden opportunities to teach or reinforce concepts are not limited to teaching mechanics, of course. A group discussion about the question "What are some problems people can have because they don't share ideas?" can lead directly into instruction on recognizing and understanding cause-and-effect relationships if the discussion discloses that some students are having trouble with these concepts. Depending upon what type of activity was going on when the question arose, the instruction could be for either a single learner or a group.

As with mini-lessons, once instruction has been given, it is usually necessary to provide follow-up practice and reinforcement. This can often be done by developing exercises related to the subject matter of the next few lessons.

The Discovery Approach

Whether instruction is planned or spontaneous, the discovery method of teaching can be useful for introducing many concepts and principles. In the discovery method, students are given several examples of a principle and are guided through questioning to figure out the principle. The following example shows how, in a series of mini-lessons, students can be led to discover the rule about dropping a final silent *e* before adding an ending that starts with a vowel.

Write the following word pairs on the chalkboard:

name	naming
save	saving
ride	riding
hope	hoping
rule	ruling

Ask the following questions about the words:

1. What is the last letter of each word in the first column?

2. Do you hear the last *e* in each word?

3. What ending has been added to the words in the second column?

4. What happens to the silent *e* in the words in the second column?

Then ask students to state the rule they have discovered so far:

When words end in silent *e*, you drop the *e* before adding *-ing* to them.

Next, give students additional silent *e* words and have them practice adding *-ing* to them.

Further instruction to discover the generalization of the rule can be done by listing silent *e* words with a mixture of endings that start with vowels (*named, ruler, wavy, nicest, natural, operator*). Ask students to identify the endings and tell whether they begin with vowels or consonants. Then add some words with endings that start with consonants (*useful, careless, lonely, amusement*). Through further questioning, students discover that the silent *e* is dropped only when adding an ending that starts with a vowel. End the discovery process by having students state the general rule:

When words end in silent *e,* you drop the *e* before adding an ending that starts with a vowel.

Give students additional word lists for practice and reinforcement as needed.

Other Useful Writing Resources

The *Challenger Teacher's Manual for Books 1–4* Revised Edition (1994) contains other useful tips for dealing with individual writing problems. In Chapter 3, writing activities are recommended for students working at various levels. In addition, the individual notes for each lesson give suggestions for topics related to the reading selection that can be used for writing activities.

Teaching the Writing Process

The steps in the writing process are discussed in detail in the next chapter. As soon as students begin to write paragraphs, you can give instruction in the writing process, and they can begin to practice the steps. Using prewriting techniques before creating any piece of writing is a very useful habit for students to develop. Sharing their writing with each other and offering helpful feedback are also useful steps in the process that they can begin to practice early. Whenever possible, fit instruction and practice of the various steps into your daily lessons. This will allow students to progress from the safety of the exercises in the writing books, with their controlled vocabulary and familiar formats and subject matter, to freer and more expressive writing.

Chapter 4

Developing Skill in the Writing Process

As students progress through the lessons in *Writing for Challenger,* they encounter exercises that take them gradually from writing simple sentences through guided writing of paragraphs to more extensive writing with less guidance. You probably will also provide additional writing opportunities that directly relate to learners' personal goals and interests. Whether working on exercises in *Writing for Challenger* or on other activities, your students will be more successful writers if they understand and use the steps in the writing process.

The writing process consists of four principal stages: prewriting, writing, revising, and editing. There are several steps in each stage. If students understand and use certain techniques in each of the four stages, writing tasks will be easier for them. As students become more proficient at using the writing process, the projects they undertake will be more interesting and rewarding, and they will find that they are able to use writing more often in their daily lives.

Stage 1: Prewriting

Planning and organizing activities make up the prewriting stage of most writing projects. The extent of prewriting will depend on the purpose of the project, but it is important for students to develop the habit of doing some prethinking and planning whenever they begin a writing assignment. Beginning with the early lessons in Book 1, students can be encouraged to think about what they plan to write before actually writing. With continual practice in class, students can internalize the prethinking and planning stage of the process and use it regularly, whether writing in or outside of class. Specific suggestions for using prewriting activities in conjunction with exercises in *Writing for Challenger* can be found in the descriptions of the individual exercises in Chapter 2.

Steps in the prewriting stage are described in detail on the pages that follow. Not all of these steps will be necessary for each writing activity. Most of them, however, should be taught and practiced whenever students do extended writing projects.

Defining the Purpose and Audience

Regardless of the type of writing to be done, there should be a clear understanding of the purpose of the writing and the audience to which it is being directed. In many exercises in *Writing for Challenger,* the purpose and audience are clearly defined for students. In most exercises, the instructions, starter questions, or other clues give a good sense of both purpose and audience. However, the *Writing for Challenger* books are controlled exercise books and do not always reflect real-world writing. You can extend writing for real-world uses by developing writing activities that are based on students' lives and needs. This will heighten student interest in writing and give them a chance to practice the entire writing process, starting with identifying the purpose and audience.

To generate the maximum interest and involvement of students, provide as many opportunities as possible for them to write about subjects that interest them and to write in formats that are useful to them.

For example, you may think that writing friendly letters is a practical way to involve students in writing, but if learning to write such letters has no recognizable value to someone, the activity becomes a meaningless exercise. The same person may need to write a letter of complaint, however, so changing the purpose and audience for the writing activity may capture the person's attention. From your standpoint, the two activities are quite similar, but for the student there is a lot of difference. Find out what actual writing needs your students have. Then the appropriate purpose and audience for a writing activity will become clear.

Brainstorming a Topic

It is important to help learners select writing topics, especially when they are first getting involved in doing open-ended writing activities. When students are going to write about a current news event, a concept being discussed in a lesson, or something related to their work or personal lives, they must choose the specific topic themselves. Deciding what to write about can often be the hardest part of getting started. To help students become independent writers, you will need to teach them a process for selecting topics.

A brainstorming session is often a good way to produce topics. All participants in a brainstorming session are free to offer ideas. If brainstorming is done with a group, write all ideas on a chalkboard or flip chart without comment. If brainstorming is done with one other person, write the ideas on a piece of paper. Neither you nor any of the students should criticize or in any way evaluate suggestions as they are being generated. Let the ideas flow. You can add some ideas of your own to the list to make the brainstorming a shared activity, but don't dominate.

After a sufficient number of topic ideas have been generated, end the brainstorming session and have students select a topic. They should eliminate from the list those ideas that do not really suit the particular activity. Ask probing questions to help students evaluate the suggestions, and cross out those that have been eliminated.

Keep in mind that at this time the task is to brainstorm topics only. Generating ideas related to the topic and organizing those ideas for writing is done later.

Initially, you should work with individuals or groups to do brainstorming. Once students have become accustomed to the process, they can work effectively in pairs or in small groups. Ultimately, they should be able to brainstorm on their own.

Generating Ideas

Once a topic has been selected, students need to generate and organize ideas related to it. Following are some techniques they may find useful for generating ideas.

Free writing. Free writing can be used as a prewriting technique. In free writing, people write down everything that comes to mind about a topic as fast as possible in a predetermined amount of time (usually five to fifteen minutes). They should write without concern for spelling, punctuation, or word selection, and they should stop for nothing. Suggest that students draw lines in place of words they can't think of and then go on. A person who runs out of ideas can write "I can't think of anything else" repeatedly until a new idea does come. The object is to keep concentrating on the topic and the task of generating ideas for the designated period of time. When the free writing is completed, the writer can select and organize the best ideas.

The reporter's questions. Reporters are taught to answer the questions *who, what, when, where, why,* and *how* when writing a story. These questions can also be used to generate ideas when a topic relates to an event that has happened or to something that someone is going to do.

Brainstorming ideas. Brainstorming can also be used to generate ideas about a specific topic. This is particularly helpful when students are working in pairs or groups, but it can also be done individually, as a variation of free writing. Tell students to list ideas, key words, and phrases that come to mind as they think about the topic. Again, they should let the ideas flow and not try to organize or evaluate them until later. The reporter's questions listed above can be used to start a brainstorming session or to stimulate additional ideas about a topic.

While the purpose, audience, and topic for writing are usually clearly defined in the exercises in *Writing for Challenger,* techniques for generating ideas can be introduced and practiced whenever students are asked to respond to personal opinion questions. For instance, in Lesson 8 of Book 1, you can ask students to tell you what they like to do at an amusement park. Jot down their ideas as they respond. This will provide them with a list of correctly spelled words and phrases that they can choose from to complete the sentence in the exercise.

Selecting and Organizing Ideas

After ideas have been generated, the best ones to use for the purpose and topic of the writing activity must be selected. Suggest that students begin by eliminating ideas that are not relevant or important. The remaining ideas can be used as the basis for writing the first draft. Students don't have to narrow the list down to only those ideas that definitely will be used. Additional ideas can be eliminated or added naturally when organizing ideas in preparation for writing.

Selecting the ideas to use is a fairly easy step of the writing process. Organizing and prioritizing the ideas is more difficult. The following are three frequently used and effective techniques for organizing ideas.

Idea mapping. Idea mapping is an informal, nonthreatening technique for organizing topic ideas before writing. An idea map is a visual representation of a writing project—a map for writing. The map can be drawn after a list of ideas has been generated and the inappropriate ideas have been eliminated. The following map illustrates the relationships of the ideas in the prewriting section of this chapter. It may help to clarify the discussion of the process that follows.

First, write the topic in a circle in the center of the page. From the list of available ideas relating to the topic, choose a main idea for each paragraph. Draw a circle branching from the topic circle for each main idea identified, leaving enough room around each to add supporting details. The order in which the main ideas are written around the circle is not important.

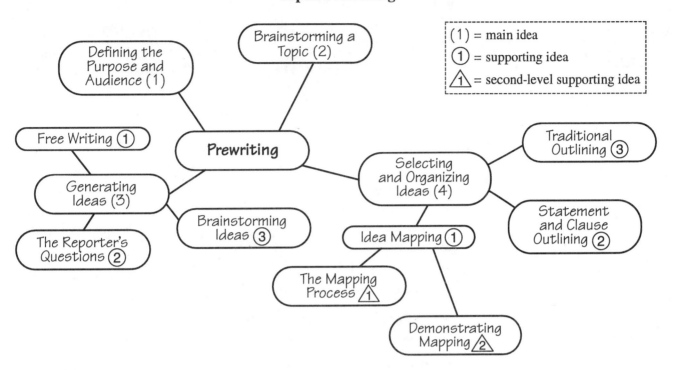

IDEA MAP
Topic: Prewriting

Defining the Purpose and Audience (1)

Brainstorming a Topic (2)

(1) = main idea
(1) = supporting idea
(1) = second-level supporting idea

Free Writing (1)

Prewriting

Traditional Outlining (3)

Generating Ideas (3)

Selecting and Organizing Ideas (4)

The Reporter's Questions (2)

Brainstorming Ideas (3)

Idea Mapping (1)

Statement and Clause Outlining (2)

The Mapping Process (1)

Demonstrating Mapping (2)

Next, choose from the brainstorming list supporting ideas, details, or arguments that relate to each main idea. Write those in circles reaching out from the main ideas. The number of supporting ideas will depend on the purpose of the writing project. A supporting idea may itself have supporting ideas. The idea map above shows the topic and three other levels of ideas.

When the map is complete, number the ideas in the order in which they will be used. Then begin with the first numbered circle and write a paragraph using the main idea and its supporting ideas. The same process is followed with the second main idea, and so on.

You can introduce idea mapping by demonstrating it on a chalkboard or flip chart before students try the technique on their own. For your demonstration, use a selection in the *Challenger* reading book or an article from a newspaper or magazine that has straightforward ideas and is well organized. Or use a list from a recent group brainstorming session.

Statement and clause outlining. Outlining is probably the most familiar and most frequently taught method of organizing ideas for writing. The statement and clause outline is an informal outlining procedure. It works particularly well if the writing project calls for the writer to support a position or make an argument for something.

In a statement and clause outline, the topic statement is written at the top of the page. Below it, all the supporting arguments are listed in the form of "because" clauses. It is also a good idea to write the arguments that might be made against a case. This helps the writer to develop counterarguments. When the list of clauses is finished, weak or irrelevant points should be eliminated. Next, the writer should number the remaining points in the order in which they will appear. The writer can then string together and flesh out the points to be made, following the numbered sequence.

For example, if some of your students wanted to write a letter of complaint to their landlord asking for regular extermination services, a statement and clause outline for that letter might look like this:

Topic Statement: The landlord should have our apartment building sprayed every month.

1. because almost every apartment has cockroaches

2. because mice live in the building

3. because two people have seen rats

4. because rats are dangerous to everyone, especially babies

5. because the tenants have tried to get rid of the roaches, mice, and rats

6. because only a professional exterminator can get rid of the roaches, mice, and rats

7. because it is the landlord's responsibility to keep the building free of insects, mice, and rats

8. because the tenants will have to file a complaint with the city if the landlord doesn't correct the problem in 30 days

The statement and clause outline is not the best tool for all topics. When demonstrating this technique, be sure to select an appropriate topic.

Traditional outlining. A traditional outline can be a tool for helping your students organize their writing, but it is probably more formal and complex than necessary for most of the writing activities that your students will do. A traditional outline for this chapter up to this point might look like this:

Developing skill in the writing process

    I. Stage 1: Prewriting

        A. Defining the purpose and audience

        B. Brainstorming a topic

        C. Generating ideas

            1. Free writing

            2. The reporter's questions

            3. Brainstorming ideas

        D. Selecting and organizing ideas

            1. Idea mapping

            2. Statement and clause outlining

            3. Traditional outlining

The techniques for generating, selecting, and organizing ideas can be introduced and practiced when students are working on the paragraph writing exercises in Books 2, 3, and 4, of *Writing for Challenger.* The guiding questions can prompt ideas to include and can suggest how ideas may be organized. After students have become familiar with organizing techniques, they might want to experiment by adding other ideas and organizing their paragraphs differently. Then they can compare finished products to see which organization seems most effective.

Stage 2: Writing a First Draft

When students have selected and organized their ideas, they are ready to write a first draft. Encourage them to write straight through to the end. They should not worry about spelling, punctuation, or the specific wording in sentences or paragraphs. Be sure they understand that they will have ample opportunity to evaluate their first drafts, reorganize them, and rewrite them. Tell students clearly that you will read the draft and help them to evaluate and reorganize it, but you will not be grading the first draft in any way.

Ask students to write on every other line of ruled paper so that the revision process will be easier. Skipping lines provides room to make changes to the first draft.

Especially for the first several writing activities, you should be on hand to offer encouragement and give suggestions. If students ask you how to spell words or to react to what they have written so far, remind them that those concerns will be addressed at a later stage.

Stage 3: Revising

Students often think that people who write for a living can simply dash off several paragraphs of perfect prose in a few minutes. The truth, of course, is that a professional writer may revise a piece eight or nine times and seldom revises anything fewer than three times.

It is important for learners with limited writing experience to realize that everyone has to do revisions to achieve a good final product. A way to prove the point is to demonstrate the revision process using a piece of your own writing. If you don't have a rough draft of some sort that is suitable to use, take a few minutes to draft a short piece on a topic that your students will have the experience and vocabulary to understand and evaluate. Use an overhead projector or write the material on a chalkboard or flip chart. Involve the students in finding problems and offering suggestions for improving the writing.

This demonstration will:

- show students what to do when evaluating, reorganizing, and revising
- avoid making anyone feel uncomfortable by using a student's writing for the demonstration
- convince students that there is nothing to fear in letting others see and participate in evaluating their writing

Evaluating the First Draft

An effective way to evaluate a first draft is to have both the writer and a second person evaluate the writing and then compare and discuss their thoughts. Students can often work in pairs or small groups to evaluate each other's first drafts. You also will need to evaluate the draft in order to provide guidance for revising it.

Using a checklist. An evaluation will bring the best results if everyone is focused on the same questions. One way to accomplish this is to provide a checklist that you and your students can follow in reacting to a first draft.

A writing revision checklist should focus on content, organization, and appropriateness of expression. For short pieces of writing, a few general questions, such as the following, should be enough to guide the evaluation:

- Is the topic clear?
- Are there enough supporting details related to the topic?

- Is the organization of the ideas clear and logical?

- Are the sentences varied in length and structure?

- Are the words varied, colorful, and appropriate?

- Does the writing do what it is intended to do?

A photocopy master titled "Writing Revision Checklist" can be found on page 29. This checklist can be used to guide evaluation of a more extensive composition.

Teacher evaluation. When students first begin to do open-ended assignments, you will probably want to evaluate their writing yourself rather than have students evaluate each other's work. Doing so allows you to give direct guidance to each person and usually is more comfortable for students who are new to the evaluation process. You should use the same writing revision checklist that they use to evaluate their own work. This way, students become accustomed to following a standard procedure.

Even when there are peer evaluators, you should continue to do your own evaluations of students' writing. You will need to identify areas of weakness so that you can work with individuals to remediate their writing problems.

When evaluating a first draft, pick one or two key areas that the student can concentrate on improving for the next draft. These areas should be related to the content or organization of the work, not to mechanical errors. Make suggestions to the writer about revisions carefully and gently, especially if a first draft needs a lot of reworking. Stress the good points. Comment on areas that have improved since the last writing assignment. Note the new vocabulary and ideas that the writer has made an effort to use. Remember, at this stage you are helping students to improve, not perfect, their drafts. There will be opportunities to work with students on additional problems later.

Peer and group evaluation. To make peer evaluation work effectively, everyone on the evaluation team, including the writer, must approach the task with the same primary objective in mind: to give positive feedback, not to criticize. You can model positive criticism to make sure this objective is met.

Be sure students are comfortable with having others see their work. Some students may need to go through the process with you a few times before they feel comfortable enough to allow their peers to do evaluations. Occasionally, a person may never feel comfortable enough to have peers participate. You should honor those feelings even as you continue to work to win the person's confidence in the process.

Revising the First Draft

After suggestions have been given during the evaluation of the first draft, students can make revisions. Like the first draft, all revisions should be double-spaced to allow for final editing. The revised draft can be evaluated using the same procedures. Writers should then decide if another intermediate revision is necessary before the editing stage. The number of revisions needed will depend not only on the quality of the writing but also on the purpose for the writing activity.

Stage 4: The Final Draft

Final Editing

When the content, organization, and expression of ideas have all been revised, the most current draft should be edited. Editing involves both evaluating the revisions already made and marking mechanical errors that need to be corrected.

Both writers and their peers should evaluate revised drafts for mechanical problems such as incorrect spelling, capitalization and punctuation errors, and missing words, as well as for content and organization.

Again, a checklist is a helpful tool for providing suggestions and recommendations to incorporate into the final draft. The following questions might be included in an editing checklist for a short writing project:

- Is the revised draft easier to understand?
- Are the topic and supporting ideas clear?
- Are the ideas organized in an effective way?
- Are all words used and spelled correctly?
- Are sentences capitalized and punctuated correctly?
- Is each sentence a complete thought?
- Are there long sentences that could be improved by making two or more sentences from them?

A photocopy master titled "Editing Checklist" that might be useful for evaluating longer writing activities can be found on page 30.

Review the corrections and changes that students recommend before a writer begins a final draft. Be positive and flexible in making your own recommendations. Request additional changes only if they are important. You can address other problems in future assignments.

Writing the Final Draft

Once the editing checklist is completed and you have given guidance for making changes, the writer should write editing changes onto the revised draft. You can then review the edited draft before the student prepares a clean, single-spaced final draft. Be sure that all writing is dated. Have students keep all of their drafts in a folder or notebook as a record of progress.

Using the Writing Process with *Writing for Challenger*

As mentioned before, the paragraph-writing strand of exercises in *Writing for Challenger* can be used to teach the steps in the writing process. In the early exercises in Book 2, you probably will want to focus your evaluation of students' writing on content and expression of ideas. Revising and editing can be introduced in conjunction with later exercises.

Use the starter questions to practice prewriting techniques. Have students answer the questions orally and put their responses into an idea map or an outline. Discuss which ideas can and cannot be put together in the same paragraph to help them see the basic logic in paragraphs.

Peer evaluation of writing can be introduced with the paragraph-writing exercises in Book 3 if you haven't done so earlier. Getting your students involved in peer evaluation while they are writing guided single paragraphs is easier than waiting until they are writing three-paragraph compositions. You may want to introduce revising at that earlier stage also, but revising can be introduced later when learners begin to write three-paragraph compositions.

After students have become comfortable with the three-paragraph format, have them begin to revise and edit their writing regularly, using both peer evaluations and yours. Help students plan their revisions. Particularly in the open-ended format, they may tend to write something altogether different instead of revising and improving what they have already written.

By teaching the writing process, you enable learners to build thinking skills as well as writing skills. For instance, the steps in the prewriting stage require brainstorming, selecting and rejecting details, and organizing. Critical thinking skills are necessary for the revision stage. Reading for meaning and evaluating material written by others, also thinking skills, are enhanced when students read and react to each other's writing.

In the sections that follow, answers are given for the exercises in *Writing for Challenger 1–4*.

Writing Revision Checklist
(to be used to react to early drafts)

	Author		Reader	
	Yes	**Needs Work**	**Yes**	**Needs Work**
Is the topic clearly stated?				
Does each paragraph have a sentence that tells clearly what the paragraph is about?				
Are there enough supporting details, examples, or reasons?				
Are all ideas related to the topic?				
Have all the important questions that readers might ask been answered?				
Is there a beginning, a middle, and an end?				
Are all ideas arranged in a logical order?				
Does the writing seem complete?				
Are there connecting words to help readers relate the ideas to each other?				
Are there some long, medium, and short sentences?				
Are there different kinds of sentences (for instance, questions or commands)?				
Have interesting, colorful, and appropriate words been chosen?				
Rather than some words being used again and again, have different words been used to express the same idea?				

Editing Checklist
(to be used to guide the final draft)

	Author		Reader	
	Yes	**Needs Work**	**Yes**	**Needs Work**
Is the topic clearly stated?				
Do all the ideas relate to the topic?				
Do added ideas make the author's meaning clearer?				
Does any new order of sentences or paragraphs improve the writing?				
Is the revised draft easier to understand?				
Is the revised draft more convincing?				
Are all words spelled correctly?				
Are all sentences punctuated correctly?				
Are capital letters used whenever necessary?				
Is each sentence a complete thought?				
Have all run-on sentences been fixed?				
Do pronouns refer clearly to someone or something?				
Are all action words used correctly?				

Lesson 1

1 Fill in the Missing Word
1. o'clock   3. late
2. fired   4. quit

2 Answer the Questions
1. Bob was late for work.
2. Eddie and Mike rode to the park with Bob.
3. Bob woke up at nine o'clock.
4. Bob hates his job.
5. Eddie did not have a job at the time.
6. Mr. Jones fired Bob.

3 Put These Sentences in Order
1. Bob was late for his job.
2. Bob hoped Mr. Jones would not fire him.
3. Mr. Jones did fire Bob.
4. Bob rode to the park with Eddie and Mike.

4 What Do You Think?
Answers vary.

5 Unscramble the Sentences
1. Bob got a ride to his job.
2. Bob rode with Eddie.

Lesson 2

1 Fill in the Missing Word
1. job   4. Eddie
2. bikes   5. hire
3. bad

2 Answer the Questions
1. Dan Rose was a friend of Bob's dad.
2. Bob had a date to see Dan Rose.
3. The job was fixing bikes.
4. Bob said he did not have to see Dan until five o'clock.
5. Eddie did not want to let his friend down.

3 Put These Sentences in Order
1. Bob said, "I hope I feel relaxed when I meet Dan."
2. Eddie said, "Let's ride around until it is time to see him."
3. Bob was relaxed by the time he got to Dan's home.
4. Dan said he would hire Bob to fix bikes.

4 What Do You Think?
Answers vary.

5 Unscramble the Sentences
1. Bob had a date to see Dan Rose.
2. The job was fixing bikes.

Lesson 3

1 Fill in the Missing Word
1. loved   4. jeep
2. bank   5. week
3. met

2 Answer the Questions
1. Kate was Eddie's girlfriend.
2. Dave had a jeep.
3. Eddie was with Mike and Dave in the jeep.
4. Dave beeped the horn so Kate would see Eddie.
5. Kate seemed mad at the beeping.
6. Eddie and Kate had fun at the lake.

3 Put These Sentences in Order
1. Eddie rode to the lake with Mike and Dave.
2. Eddie made Dave beep the horn.
3. Kate loved Eddie at first sight!
4. Kate rode off with Eddie in Dave's jeep.

4 What Do You Think?
Answers vary.

5 Unscramble the Sentences
1. Eddie hoped that Kate loved him.
2. She rode off with him in Dave's jeep.

Lesson 4

1 Answer the Questions
1. Kate lived with her aunt.
2. Louise was Kate's aunt.
3. Kate wanted to bake the cake without help.
4. Kate dug a hole behind her home and put the cake in it.

2 Put These Sentences in Order
1. Kate wanted to bake a cake for Eddie.
2. Aunt Louise said she would help Kate.
3. Kate refused her Aunt Louise's help.
4. The cake looked like a joke and was bad.
5. Kate put the cake in a hole she dug.

3 Unscramble the Sentences
1. Kate didn't know how to bake.
2. Kate ate a bite of the cake.
3. She fed the cake to the cat.
4. The cat hated the cake.
5. Kate was mad at herself.

4 What Do You Think?
Answers vary.

Lesson 5

1 Add Another Word

1. mitt
2. Ben
3. home
4. hug

2 Answer the Questions

1. Kate's friends liked to talk to her Aunt Louise.
2. Bob went to see Aunt Louise after work.
3. Aunt Louise was fixing beef for dinner.
4. Bob talked to women who needed to have bikes fixed.

3 What Do You Think?

Answers may vary.

1. she talked to him about his problems.
2. she listened to them.

4 Unscramble the Sentences

1. I have a problem at work.
2. Would you like to have dinner with us?
3. It was fun to talk and joke with Aunt Louise.

5 Personal Questions

Answers vary.

Lesson 6

1 Fill in the Missing Word

1. sick
2. track
3. phone
4. refund
5. ducks
6. won

2 Answer the Questions

Answers may vary.

1. Eddie wanted to get his girlfriend Kate a box of red roses.
2. Eddie's friends didn't have money to lend him.
3. Eddie hopped on a bus and went to the track.
4. The woman next to Eddie gave him a few hints on betting.

3 What Do You Think?

Answers may vary.

1. he won two races at the track.
2. he was too greedy and his luck ran out.

4 Put These Sentences in Order

1. Eddie got to the track.
2. He bet the money he had and won.
3. Eddie made up his mind to bet again.
4. His horse limped in last, and that was the end of Eddie's money.

5 Personal Questions

Answers vary.

Lesson 7

1 Add Another Word

1. dozed
2. dunk
3. looked
4. sang

2 Answer the Questions

Answers may vary.

1. Dave wanted to sink back into the bed when the clock rang.
2. Dave needed to take money out of the bank so he could go downtown and look for a new car.
3. Dave needed a new car because he had junked his jeep.
4. The cat banged into a box of fuses.

3 What Do You Think?

Answers may vary.

1. he didn't want to look for a new car.
2. Dave put the jam away.

4 Unscramble the Sentences

1. Dave had to get to the bank by nine o'clock.
2. The jam pot hit the sink with a bang.
3. Dave wiped up the jam and went back to bed.

5 Personal Questions

Answers vary.

Lesson 8

1 Fill in the Missing Word

1. fuss
2. amusement
3. huge
4. keeled
5. ago
6. stayed

2 Add Another Word

1. Jack
2. beef
3. male
4. hum
5. games
6. home

3 Answer the Questions

Answers may vary.

1. Aunt Louise and Jack rode to the amusement park in a cab.
2. Aunt Louise was happy again once they were at the amusement park.
3. The rides were ten cents years ago.

4 Put These Sentences in Order

1. Jack and Aunt Louise rode in a cab.
2. Aunt Louise was getting mad.
3. Jack said that they should go home.

5 What Do You Think?

Answers vary.

Lesson 9

1 Fill in the Missing Word
1. guy   3. joy
2. birthday   4. myself

2 Choose the Right Word
1. safely   3. jack
2. quickly

3 Unscramble the Sentences
1. Bob is going to be twenty-four on Wednesday.
2. They had only six bucks to get something nice.

4 Answer the Questions
Answers may vary.
1. Bob's friends didn't have any money because payday wasn't until Friday.
2. Kate didn't bake the cake because Eddie wanted her aunt to bake it.
3. Dave said Bob's friends should buy him some toys.
4. They all got into Mike's car and went downtown.
5. Yes, Linda went downtown with them.

5 What Do You Think?
Answers vary.

Lesson 10

1 Fill in the Missing Word
1. ditch   3. wrong
2. write   4. fight

2 Choose the Right Word
1. numb   3. right
2. gone

3 Unscramble the Sentences
1. He knew this guy was just a bum.
2. Eddie was happy that he was safe.

4 Answer the Questions
Answers may vary.
1. They had a date to see a movie.
2. The man asked Eddie for a match.
3. The man waved a knife in Eddie's face.
4. Eddie swung his right hand and knocked the knife from the man's hand.
5. He put his foot on the gas too quickly.
6. He was limping a little bit.

5 Personal Questions
Answers vary.

Lesson 11

1 Fill in the Missing Word
1. women   3. purse
2. work

2 Choose the Right Word
1. care   3. firmly
2. birthday

3 Answer the Questions
Answers may vary.
1. Mary went to Aunt Louise's because her mom and dad had not come home from work yet.
2. Mary's dad says, "There's no harm in asking."
3. Aunt Louise and Eddie sat and laughed when Jack got mad.

4 Put These Sentences in Order
1. Mary asked if she could stay with Aunt Louise for a while.
2. Aunt Louise said, "I think tonight is going to be my lucky night."
3. Mary played cards with Jack, Eddie, and Aunt Louise.
4. Aunt Louise and Mary won just about all the hands.
5. Jack was mad when Mary left.

5 Complete the Sentences
Answers may vary.
1. it was just starting to get dark.
2. playing hide-and-seek.
3. little girls around when he played cards.
4. it was time for her to go home.

Lesson 12

1 Fill in the Missing Word
1. paid   3. join
2. lie

2 Choose the Right Word
1. loudly   3. join
2. foot

3 Answer the Questions
Answers may vary.
1. Kate didn't have the money to buy a new coat.
2. Eddie wanted to celebrate his new job.
3. Kate was sorry she shouted at Eddie.

4 **Put These Sentences in Order**

1. Kate was in a bad mood today.
2. Eddie came into the room.
3. Kate was in no mood to put up with Eddie's bad temper.
4. Eddie said maybe Bob would celebrate with him.
5. Kate said she was sorry.

5 **What Do You Think?**

Answers vary.

Lesson 13

1 **Fill in the Missing Words**

1. fair/hair
2. part/dark
3. smart/aid
4. dear/year

2 **Answer the Questions**

Answers may vary.
1. Dave had made up his mind to take a class at night school.
2. Dave could pick up some hints on how to paint better.
3. Dave was painting a picture of a pear.
4. Joan's pear looked like a box.
5. Dave felt that night school was going to be a lot more fun than he thought it would be.

3 **Unscramble the Sentences**

1. Dave had failed art in high school.
2. A lovely woman was painting near Dave.
3. Dave said he had been painting for years.
4. I would like to buy you a cup of coffee.

4 **Complete the Sentences**

Answers may vary.
1. he was getting tired of just going to work, looking at television, hanging out with his friends, or seeing Linda in the evenings.
2. tear it up and forget all about night school.
3. Joan said it really looked like a pear.
4. he had been painting for years.

Lesson 14

1 **Choose the Right Word**

1. belt   4. fill
2. pull   5. yell
3. wild   6. cold

2 **Put These Sentences in Order**

1. Eddie stopped at Jack's house to give him some film.
2. Eddie could hear Jack laughing loudly in the den.
3. Eddie could see Jack wasn't reading a book.
4. Eddie asked Jack what was so funny.
5. Jack handed Eddie his phone bill.

3 **Answer the Questions**

Answers may vary.
1. Jack was paying his bills and laughing.
2. Jack's phone bill was for only ten cents.
3. Eddie was so happy to have a job that he didn't mind paying bills.

4 **Fill in the Missing Words**

1. useful/useless
2. harmful/harmless
3. helpful/helpless
4. careless/careful

5 **What Do You Think?**

Answers vary.

Lesson 15

1 **Fill in the Missing Words**

1. loud/loudest
2. big/biggest
3. lovely/loveliest
4. lucky/luckiest

2 **Answer the Questions**

Answers may vary.
1. Kate wanted to buy a new chair for her room.
2. Kate said, "You can't boss us around like that."
3. The manager said Kate could have anything in the store that she wanted.
4. He thought the masked men could have fired the gun at her.

3 **Unscramble the Sentences**

1. Two men were holding up the store.
2. Kate marched toward the masked men.
3. Kate fired the gun at a lamp.
4. The lamp burst into a million bits.

4 **Complete the Sentences**

Answers may vary.
1. she would end up buying something cheap.
2. hear a pin drop.
3. "Reach for the sky, you two."
4. the two men dashed out of the store as if they were being chased by real cops.
5. one of those jerks had fired at you? Then where would you be?"

Lesson 16

1 Put These Sentences in Order
1. Bob slammed his hand in the car door.
2. He saw that his thumb was cut.
3. Bob asked June to go out Saturday night.
4. Bob said they could talk about the good old days.

2 Answer the Questions
Answers may vary.
1. Bob wrapped his hand in an old cloth.
2. Dr. Chase's place was in the middle of the next block.
3. June Baker was the nurse at Dr. Chase's.
4. June thought Bob's hand looked bad, but the rest of him looked just fine.
5. Bob and June planned to go out Saturday night.

3 Fill in the Missing Words
1. sunshine/sundown
2. baseball/football
3. cake/cupcakes
4. weekends/workweek

4 What Do You Think?
Answers vary.

Lesson 17

1 Choose the Right Word
1. shirt
2. brave
3. prize
4. free
5. cleaner

2 Answer the Questions
Answers may vary.
1. Running into June at Dr. Chase's was like a dream come true.
2. Dan Rose yelled because Bob wasn't strong enough to go back to work yet.
3. Dan was upset because his prize worker was out sick.
4. Bob planned to take June to the Steak House for dinner.
5. Bob froze in his tracks because he didn't have any money.

3 Unscramble the Sentences
1. Bob was proud of his clothes.
2. Bob had to decide where to take June.
3. Bob put on his jacket to go downtown.
4. Bob didn't have a dime to his name.

4 Complete the Sentences
Answers may vary.
1. he was going out with June that night.
2. his hand was all wrapped up.
3. what June would want to do.
4. he had missed work yesterday.

Lesson 18

1 Choose the Right Word
1. sneeze
2. wheel
3. three
4. snake
5. thin

2 Answer the Questions
Answers may vary.
1. Billy smashed Jack in the chest with a toy.
2. Jack thought Billy might need a good spanking.
3. Jack said that he was over six feet tall and that Billy was maybe three feet tall.
4. Billy was sitting calmly on the floor and playing with his toy trucks.
5. She said, "You sure do have a way with kids."

3 Put These Sentences in Order
1. Mary's mother and father wanted to take Mary to a play.
2. Mary's mother told Jack to be firm with Billy.
3. Billy wheeled his bike into the room and rolled it right into Jack's legs.
4. Jack asked Billy if he had learned about numbers in math.
5. Billy was sitting calmly on the floor.

4 What Do You Think?
Answers vary.

Lesson 19

1 Choose the Right Word
1. shrink
2. scar
3. beside
4. splint
5. Christmas

2 Answer the Questions
Answers may vary.
1. She heard the sound of screeching tires.
2. She saw a car strike a tree.
3. They were talking and taking notes.
4. She tripped over some strips of chrome that were all over the ground.
5. She fell on top of the man she was trying to help.

BOOK 1

3 **Unscramble the Sentences**
1. Kate dashed outside to help.
2. Kate was getting more and more upset.
3. She sprinted across the street to help.
4. Kate cared about these poor men.
5. The man gave her a very surprised look.

4 **Complete the Sentences**
Answers may vary.
1. called the police.
2. streaming down his left arm.
3. all over the man on the ground.
4. the fake blood on the movie star.

Lesson 20

1 **Fill in the Missing Words**
1. Pork chops/roast beef
2. pancakes/corn flakes
3. candy bar/ice cream cone

2 **Put These Sentences in Order**
1. Bob asked Aunt Louise to lend him some money.
2. Bob called June and explained what happened.
3. Bob said, "Maybe we can go out next week."
4. June said she would fix a nice meal.
5. June said, "I'm really glad to see you."

3 **Answer the Questions**
Answers may vary.
1. He had no money and wanted Aunt Louise to lend him some.
2. He had a date and hadn't had a chance to pick up his paycheck.

3. She was mending a blouse to wear that night.
4. June asked Bob to come over and eat dinner at her home.

4 **What Do You Think?**
Answers vary.

Review

1 **Fill in the Missing Word**
1. safely   5. almost
2. celebrate 6. remind
3. surprise   7. useful
4. next

2 **Unscramble the Sentences**
1. I pay cash for my food.
2. Mary takes the train to work.
3. A loud knock on the door woke me up.

3 **Put These Sentences in Order**
1. Joan was driving her car downtown.
2. She was driving very fast in the rain.
3. Her car began to slip.
4. Joan crashed into another car.
5. Joan was lucky that nobody was hurt.

4 **What Do You Think?**
Answers vary.

5 **Personal Questions**
Answers vary.

BOOK 2

Lesson 1

1 **Choose the Right Word**
1. children 4. over
2. draw   5. mouth
3. touch   6. sense

2 **Personal Questions**
Answers vary.

3 **Unscramble the Sentences**
1. June Clark had the worst sneezing fit.
2. Most people cover their noses when they sneeze.

4 **Combine the Sentences**
1. Somebody may hear you sneezing and say, "God bless you."
2. June Clark was seventeen years old when she had the worst sneezing fit ever recorded. *or* June Clark had the worst sneezing fit ever recorded when she was seventeen years old.

5 **What Do You Think?**
Answers vary.

Lesson 2

1 **Choose the Right Word**
1. catcall   3. paws
2. barking   4. cats

2 Unscramble the Sentences

1. Cats like to have their own way.
2. Cats have sharp senses of smell and hearing.

3 What Do You Think?

Answers vary.

4 Combine the Sentences

1. Dogs and cats make good pets.
2. A doctor who lived on the West Coast died in 1963.
3. The doctor left his money to his two cats in his will. *or* In his will, the doctor left his money to his two cats.

5 Personal Questions

Answers vary.

Lesson 3

1 Choose the Right Word

1. ten   3. eighty
2. hundred   4. thousand

2 Unscramble the Sentences

1. Seven is a lucky number for many people.
2. Cells in the human body are renewed every seven years.

3 What Do You Think?

Answers vary.

4 Combine the Sentences

1. One woman quit smoking and saved $1,500 in seven years.
2. There are seven days in a week and (there are) seven deadly sins.
3. By law, a person who is missing for seven years is recorded as dead.

5 Personal Questions

Answers vary.

Lesson 4

1 Choose the Right Word

1. drink   4. pubs
2. quarts   5. English
3. pints   6. react

2 Combine the Sentences

1. You can tell time in hours and seconds.
2. The word *ugly* is the opposite of the word *cute*.
3. Eddie always walks home from work the same way.
4. The United States is big, but the world is bigger.

3 What Do You Think?

Answers vary.

4 Unscramble the Sentences

1. The people on the *Mayflower* would have gone further south.
2. Sunlight turns beer cloudy and gives it a funny smell.

5 Personal Questions

Answers vary.

Lesson 5

1 Choose the Right Word

1. pepper   4. person
2. chain   5. letters
3. wrote

2 Unscramble the Sentences

1. The lover did not write the letter himself.
2. The lover hired a scribe to write the letter.
3. The words were written over and over.
4. This must have been a boring job.

3 What Do You Think?

Answers vary.

4 Combine the Sentences

1. A scribe is a person who writes for a living.
2. The lover stayed there and said "I love you" 1,875,000 times.

5 Personal Questions

Answers vary.

Lesson 6

1 Use These Words in Sentences

Answers vary.

2 Personal Questions

Answers vary.

3 Combine the Sentences

1. Anne had a checkbook that was easy to use.
2. John had a girlfriend, and her name (whose name) was Linda.
3. Shortstop is a difficult position to play in baseball.
4. Dan said, "Please give me some gingerbread and milk."

4 What Do You Think?

Answers vary.

Lesson 7

1 Unscramble the Sentences

1. There are hidden pouches under a skunk's tail.
2. Each pouch has enough liquid for six rounds.
3. It takes a week to form more liquid.

2 Combine the Sentences

1. The problem that looked hard was really easy to do.
2. Sometimes I forget important things, but I remember them later.
3. Mary saved money buying a used car, but she still spent a lot.

3 Use These Words in Sentences

Answers vary.

4 Personal Questions

Answers vary.

Lesson 8

1 Choose the Right Word

1. hatch
2. shell
3. peeping
4. chicken
5. clutch

2 What Do You Think?

Answers vary.

3 Put These Sentences in Order

1. Eggs are laid at one time.
2. Air gets into the eggs.
3. The chicks peck against the shells.
4. The sounds are heard by the other chicks.
5. The eggs hatch within a few hours of each other.

4 Personal Questions

Answers vary.

Lesson 9

1 Combine the Sentences

1. Gold was found on land owned by John A. Sutter.
2. The real gold rush began in 1849 when 100,000 men rushed to California.

2 Unscramble the Sentences

1. His word was as good as gold.
2. People thought there was a land rich in gold called El Dorado.

3 What Do You Think?

Answers vary.

4 Use These Words in Sentences

Answers vary.

5 Personal Questions

Answers vary.

Lesson 10

1 Choose the Right Word

1. through
2. sport
3. stuck
4. rhyme

2 Unscramble the Sentences

1. Mother Goose rhymes have been around for hundreds of years.
2. One queen of England loved to tease her lords.

3 What Do You Think?

Answers vary.

4 Put These Sentences in Order

1. The people who served the queen had nicknames.
2. A lady-in-waiting was called "Spoon."
3. The "Dish" and the "Spoon" ran off to get married.
4. Somebody made up a rhyme about the "Dish" and the "Spoon."

5 Personal Questions

Answers vary.
Note: Negative responses are acceptable (e.g., I don't know anyone who likes to make up rhymes).

Lesson 11

1 Use These Words in Sentences

Answers vary.

2 Combine the Sentences

1. Most dreaming takes place during the fourth stage of sleep, which is called REM.
2. During REM, the deepest sleep, the body is very limp.
3. We need to move during the time we sleep so we will not get sick.

3 What Do You Think?

Answers vary.

4 Complete These Paragraphs

Answers vary.

Lesson 12

1 Choose the Right Word
1. sunny
2. noisy
3. snappy
4. wavy
5. buddy

2 What Do You Think?
Answers vary.

3 Put These Sentences in Order
1. The drones mate with a young queen.
2. The queen lays her eggs.
3. In the fall, the honey flow is over.
4. The drones starve to death.

4 Complete These Paragraphs
Answers vary.

Lesson 13

1 Use These Words in Sentences
Answers vary.

2 What Do You Think?
Answers vary.

3 Unscramble the Sentences
1. Handwriting experts look at many factors.
2. The slant of the letters tells about the writer.

4 Combine the Sentences
1. Yesterday, I paid the bill that is due tomorrow.
2. The young woman won the race, but the older woman also did very well.

5 Complete These Paragraphs
Answers vary.

Lesson 14

1 Choose the Right Word
1. kept
2. diver
3. wouldn't
4. nowhere
5. flood

2 What Do You Think?
Answers vary.

3 Put These Sentences in Order
1. The slaves dreamed about freedom.
2. The War Between the States started.
3. The slaves were set free in 1863.
4. An ex-slave wrote a story about her life.

4 Complete These Paragraphs
Answers vary.

Lesson 15

1 Use These Words in Sentences
Answers vary.

2 What Do You Think?
Answers vary.

3 Unscramble the Sentences
1. Hold Fast is the name of a kind of barbed wire.
2. Barbed wire swizzle sticks were sold to a store.
3. Some kinds of barbed wire are no longer around.

4 Combine the Sentences
1. The doctor uses wire cutters to cut off a strand of wire.
2. Some rare barbed wire may sell for forty dollars a strand.

5 Complete These Paragraphs
Answers vary.

Lesson 16

1 Choose the Right Word
1. bank
2. which
3. damp
4. sweater
5. lost

2 What Do You Think?
Answers vary.

3 Put These Sentences in Order
1. Whales used to walk on land.
2. Whales left the land to live in the water.
3. Whales became shaped like fish.
4. Whales are hunted and are being killed off.

4 Complete These Paragraphs
Answers vary.

Lesson 17

1 Use These Words in Sentences
Answers vary.

2 What Do You Think?
Answers vary.

BOOK 2

3 Unscramble the Sentences

1. Black Bart's real first name was Charles.
2. He broke a stick from a bush to use as a gun.

4 Combine the Sentences

1. He always laid careful plans, which he kept to himself.
2. He knew the driver(,) and (he) thought he'd give him a scare.

5 Complete These Paragraphs

Answers vary.

Lesson 18

1 Choose the Right Word

1. billion	3. solid
2. slowly	4. basins

2 What Do You Think?

Answers vary.

3 Unscramble the Sentences

1. The flaming gases cooled and turned into liquid.
2. The earth's outer shell changed to a solid state.
3. The rains fell for hundreds of years.
4. Simple, one-celled forms of life began in the oceans.
5. There was no life on the land for millions of years.

4 Complete This Paragraph

Answers vary.

Lesson 19

1 Use These Words in Sentences

Answers vary.

2 Combine the Sentences

1. The convicts would push the oar, dip it into the water, and pull with all their might.
2. Until the end of his days, a convict lived with the men in his gang. *or* A convict lived with the men in his gang until the end of his days.

3 Unscramble the Sentences

1. A convict on the galleys was no longer a man.
2. Life on board a galley at sea was a living hell.

4 What Do You Think?

Answers vary.

5 Complete This Paragraph

Answers vary.

Lesson 20

1 Use These Words in Sentences

Answers vary.

2 What Do You Think?

Answers vary.

3 Put These Sentences in Order

1. George Washington was born on February 11.
2. Men tried to kidnap Washington in order to kill him.
3. His friends had to lend him money to go to New York.
4. He served two terms as president.

4 Complete These Paragraphs

Answers vary.

Review

1 Unscramble the Sentences

1. It hit him like a ton of bricks.
2. Don't wear your heart on your sleeve.
3. Don't put all your eggs in one basket.
4. Don't count your chickens until they are hatched.

2 What Do You Think?

Answers vary.

3 Put These Sentences in Order

1. Mike drove two of his friends to a party.
2. Mike drank a number of beers at the party.
3. Mike gave his car keys to a friend who wasn't drinking.
4. Mike's friend drove everyone home from the party.

4 Combine the Sentences

1. Sixty people went to the dance, and they all had a good time.
2. Teachers help people learn, but people must learn things for themselves.
3. Eating good food, getting enough sleep, and working out are things you can do to take care of yourself.

5 Complete These Paragraphs

Answers vary.

BOOK 2

Lesson 1

1 Use These Words in Sentences
Answers vary.

2 What Do You Think?
Answers vary.

3 Combine the Sentences
1. I put the dirty dishes in a dishpan and then washed them.
2. Today's newspaper had a story about a plan that backfired.
3. The city will fix the broken sidewalk in front of my house.
4. Many workers carry in their toolboxes the tools they need to do their jobs.

4 Complete These Paragraphs
Answers vary.

Lesson 2

1 Use These Words in Sentences
Answers vary.

2 What Do You Think?
Answers vary.

3 Put These Sentences in Order
1. Steven was standing on his head.
2. Jerome was feasting on beef stew.
3. Jerome said he did not think Steven was crazy.
4. Steven treated Jerome to a steak dinner.

4 Complete These Paragraphs
Answers vary.

Lesson 3

1 Use These Words in Sentences
Answers vary.

2 What Do You Think?
Answers vary.

3 Combine the Sentences
1. Divers use flashlights to see in deep water.
2. You can use these folders to file your reports.
3. Students use notebooks to write down important information.
4. Swimmers use towels to dry (themselves) off when they come out of the pool.

4 Complete These Paragraphs
Answers vary.

Lesson 4

1 Use These Words in Sentences
Answers vary.

2 What Do You Think?
Answers vary.

3 Put These Sentences in Order
1. Jerome let the phone ring eight times.
2. Ginger asked Jerome if he was coming over.
3. "I always come over to your place," complained Jerome.
4. Ginger hung up while Jerome was still talking.

4 Complete These Paragraphs
Answers vary.

Lesson 5

1 Use These Words in Sentences
Answers vary.

2 What Do You Think?
Answers vary.

3 Combine the Sentences
1. Anne was madly in love with Ben and wanted to marry him. *or* Anne, who was madly in love with Ben, wanted to marry him.
2. The boxer swung wildly, slipped, and fell against the ropes.
3. John had been away a lot lately, so we hadn't seen him for a while. *or* Because John had been away a lot lately, we hadn't seen him for a while.

4 Complete These Paragraphs
Answers vary.

Lesson 6

1 Use These Words in Sentences
Answers vary.

2 What Do You Think?
Answers vary.

3 Put These Sentences in Order
1. Jerome thought about snatching a can of blue paint.
2. Jerome reached for the can.
3. Five gallons of blue paint poured over him.
4. Tony laughed so hard that he nearly slipped on the paint.

BOOK 3

4 **Complete These Paragraphs**

Answers vary.

Lesson 7

1 **Use These Words in Sentences**

Answers vary.

2 **What Do You Think?**

Answers vary.

3 **Combine the Sentences**

1. Steven had a cold and didn't feel well, but he went to his yoga class anyway.
2. Holly told Steven he should not eat sugar because it makes people grouchy and restless.
3. Holly went to the yoga class for exercise and because it made her feel peaceful and more relaxed.

4 **Write a Paragraph**

Answers vary.

Lesson 8

1 **Use These Words in Sentences**

Answers vary.

2 **What Do You Think?**

Answers vary.

3 **Put These Sentences in Order**

1. Gail slouched against Ginger's doorway.
2. "Is it okay if I stay here for a day or two?" asked Gail.
3. "My father lost his temper," Gail said.
4. "You know very well your father's proud of his job," said Ginger.
5. "Go wash your face, and I'll fix you some breakfast," Ginger said.

4 **Write a Paragraph**

Answers vary.

Lesson 9

1 **Use These Words in Sentences**

Answers vary.

2 **What Do You Think?**

Answers vary.

3 **Combine the Sentences**

1. I left the frozen beef out to thaw and then used it to make a stew.
2. Bob has written a book about dogs that is selling well.
3. Joyce stopped to loosen the straps on her backpack because they were too tight.

4 **Write a Paragraph**

Answers vary.

Lesson 10

1 **Use These Words in Sentences**

Answers vary.

2 **What Do You Think?**

Answers vary.

3 **Put These Sentences in Order**

1. Jerome threw his laundry in the trunk of his car.
2. Jerome found Holly at the laundromat.
3. Jerome told Holly that Ginger should say she is sorry.
4. Holly said that Jerome is a jerk.
5. Jerome said women stick together like glue.

4 **Write a Paragraph**

Answers vary.

Lesson 11

1 **Use These Words in Sentences**

Answers vary.

2 **What Do You Think?**

Answers vary.

3 **Combine the Sentences**

1. I don't recall my first party, but I remember my first dance and my first date.
2. Sam often sounds edgy the first time he talks to a woman because women make him nervous.
3. Mike doesn't like to brag about things he does well, but Mary wants people to know how good Mike is, so she boasts for him.

4 **Write a Paragraph**

Answers vary.

Lesson 12

1 **Use These Words in Sentences**

Answers vary.

BOOK 3

2 What Do You Think?

Answers vary.

3 Put These Sentences in Order

1. Steven bought buttered popcorn.
2. The players came onto the field.
3. The man next to Steven bumped him.
4. Buttered popcorn spilled all over Steven.
5. Holly said, "The game is starting."

4 Write a Paragraph

Answers vary.

Lesson 13

1 Use These Words in Sentences

Answers vary.

2 What Do You Think?

Answers vary.

3 Combine the Sentences

1. Jerome had a scheme that involved Tony and Ginger.
2. Jerome bought bug spray, swept the cobwebs from the ceiling, and cleaned the carpet.
3. Anne Clark, who was at the party, asked Jerome to dance, but he waved her away.

4 Write a Paragraph

Answers vary.

Lesson 14

1 Use These Words in Sentences

Answers vary.

2 What Do You Think?

Answers vary.

3 Put These Sentences in Order

1. Tony bought a small house.
2. Mrs. Darkpill complained about the chestnut tree.
3. Tony heard the sound of a buzz saw.
4. Tony yelled at Mrs. Darkpill's kids.
5. Mrs. Darkpill called the police.

4 Write a Paragraph

Answers vary.

Lesson 15

1 Use These Words in Sentences

Answers vary.

2 What Do You Think?

Answers vary.

3 Combine the Sentences

1. Last month Gail had a baby girl that (who) weighed seven pounds, eleven ounces.
2. I take weekly dancing lessons that last one hour.
3. I went to the store yesterday and bought one quart of milk and a pint of soda.

4 Write a Paragraph

Answers vary.

Lesson 16

1 Use These Words in Sentences

Answers vary.

2 What Do You Think?

Answers vary.

3 Combine the Sentences

1. The elbow, knee, and wrist are joints in the body.
2. We have a new bathroom with a towel rack and a shower.
3. Martin, who is a good bowler, is on a (bowling) team that bowls every Thursday.

4 Write a Paragraph

Answers vary.

Lesson 17

1 Use These Words in Sentences

Answers vary.

2 What Do You Think?

Answers vary.

3 Put These Sentences in Order

1. Tony shut off the alarm.
2. Tony told Mr. Dennis he was sick.
3. Tony went to the clothing sale at the men's store.
4. Tony chose two pairs of slacks to try on.
5. Tony told the person in the fitting booth to hurry up.
6. Mr. Dennis fired Tony.

4 Write a Paragraph

Answers vary.

BOOK 3

Lesson 18

1 Use These Words in Sentences
Answers vary.

2 What Do You Think?
Answers vary.

3 Combine the Sentences
1. The carpenter needed some nails and a saw, but she had a drill. *or* The carpenter had a drill, but she needed some nails and a saw.
2. A fisherman uses a rod, hooks, and bait for fishing.
3. A baker uses a rolling pin to roll out dough that is put in pie plates.

4 Write a Paragraph
Answers vary.

Lesson 19

1 Use These Words in Sentences
Answers vary.

2 What Do You Think?
Answers vary.

3 Put These Sentences in Order
1. Jerome decided to see Ginger in person.
2. Jerome went to the club where Ginger was singing.
3. Jerome sat at a table near the band.
4. Ginger felt Jerome's stare and looked up.
5. Jerome said he missed Ginger very much.
6. Ginger sang "September Song."

4 Write a Paragraph
Answers vary.

Lesson 20

1 Use These Words in Sentences
Answers vary.

2 What Do You Think?
Answers vary.

3 Combine the Sentences
1. Bob has a passport from England with his picture in it. *or* Bob has an English passport with his picture in it.
2. The story of the flight of the Jews from Egypt, which is told in the Bible, is remembered each year during Passover.
3. I carry heavy gear for camping in a knapsack on my back. *or* I carry heavy camping gear in a knapsack on my back.

4 Write a Paragraph
Answers vary.

Review

1 Combine the Sentences
1. Ginger finally painted her apartment blue and hung new curtains.
2. Steven practiced yoga every day and got so good that he became a yoga instructor.
3. Holly got food from the refrigerator, cooked it, and ate her dinner in thirty minutes. *or* In thirty minutes, Holly got food from the refrigerator, cooked it, and ate it.

2 What Do You Think?
Answers vary.

3 Put These Sentences in Order
1. Tony drove his car to work.
2. Tony had a blowout as he drove.
3. Tony was fixing his flat tire when a police car stopped.
4. The policeman waited while Tony changed the tire.
5. Tony thanked the policeman for keeping other cars from hitting him.
6. Tony was only ten minutes late for his new job.

4 Write Paragraphs
Answers vary.

BOOK 3

Lesson 1

1 Use These Words in Sentences
Answers vary.

2 What Do You Think?
Answers vary.

3 Put These Sentences in Order
1. The heart is really two pumps in one.
2. The right side pumps blood into the lungs.
3. The left side collects blood from the lungs.
4. Then the left side of the heart pumps blood to the body.
5. Veins bring the blood back into the heart.

4 Write a Paragraph
Answers vary.

Lesson 2

1 Use These Words in Sentences
Answers vary.

2 What Do You Think?
Answers vary.

3 Combine the Sentences
1. Babe Ruth was a hero who didn't live or act like a hero.
2. The Yankees tried to get Ruth to act more like a hero by chewing him out and benching him. *or* The Yankees chewed Ruth out and benched him, trying to get him to act more like a hero.
3. Ruth was only at peace with himself when he was pitching a ball or hitting the ball with a bat.

4 Write a Paragraph
Answers vary.

Lesson 3

1 Use These Words in Sentences
Answers vary.

2 What Do You Think?
Answers vary.

3 Put These Sentences in Order
1. A man drove forty-five miles to a Pueblo Indian dance.
2. Only a few townspeople were there.
3. Then a few Pueblo Indians strolled in.
4. The Pueblos didn't know when the dance would start.
5. The dance began at two o'clock in the morning.

4 Write a Paragraph
Answers vary.

Lesson 4

1 Use These Words in Sentences
Answers vary.

2 What Do You Think?
Answers vary.

3 Combine the Sentences
1. Some people think insects should be wiped out because they sting people and animals and (they) harm forests.
2. Some insects are food for other kinds of insects or for other animals, and many insects help plants to grow.
3. Insects are cold-blooded animals that move very quickly when it is hot but become more tired when it is cold.

4 Write a Paragraph
Answers vary.

Lesson 5

1 Use These Words in Sentences
Answers vary.

2 What Do You Think?
Answers vary.

3 Put These Sentences in Order
1. A study was made of people watching a movie.
2. The words EAT POPCORN were flashing very fast on the movie screen.
3. The people could not tell this was happening.
4. However, the people's brains recorded the EAT POPCORN signs.
5. During intermission, nearly everyone rushed out to buy popcorn.

4 Write a Paragraph
Answers vary.

Lesson 6

1 Use These Words in Sentences
Answers vary.

2 What Do You Think?
Answers vary.

BOOK 4

3 Combine the Sentences

1. There is life on Earth that depends on a bright star called the sun. *or* All life on Earth depends on the sun, which is a bright star.
2. All living things are part of a process called the food chain, which starts with green plants that make food with the help of sunlight.
3. People long ago worshipped the sun as a god and offered prayers and gifts to the sun god.

4 Write a Paragraph

Answers vary.

Lesson 7

1 Use These Words in Sentences

Answers vary.

2 What Do You Think?

Answers vary.

3 Put These Sentences in Order

1. As a small child, Edison was known for asking questions.
2. When Al was seven, his family moved to Michigan.
3. Al upset his teacher with all his questions.
4. Al overheard the teacher say he was crazy.
5. Al told his mother what the teacher said.
6. Al's mother took him out of school and taught him herself.

4 Write a Three-Paragraph Summary

Answers vary.

Lesson 8

1 Use These Words in Sentences

Answers vary.

2 What Do You Think?

Answers vary.

3 Combine the Sentences

1. Guests brought their own knives, used them at mealtime, wiped them off, and stuck them back into their belts.
2. In 1100, forks were first used in Italy by a rich man's wife because she thought people looked like animals when they ate with their hands.
3. As people started to use knives and forks, they made up rules about how to set a table, such as where to put knives and spoons.

4 Write a Three-Paragraph Summary

Answers vary.

Lesson 9

1 Use These Words in Sentences

Answers vary.

2 What Do You Think?

Answers vary.

3 Put These Sentences in Order

1. Order milkshake.
2. Bite off one end of paper that covers straw.
3. Put straw in milkshake.
4. Suck on straw, and place finger over top of straw.
5. Lift straw out of shake.
6. Put bottom end in mouth, release finger, and swallow.

4 Write Paragraphs

Answers vary.

Lesson 10

1 Use These Words in Sentences

Answers vary.

2 What Do You Think?

Answers vary.

3 Combine the Sentences

1. A baker stepped outside, looked upward, and saw a strange glow in the sky that looked like a shining disc.
2. The French baker saw one gleaming disc that moved very fast, but the American saw nine discs.
3. Most people who have been hired to find out whether or not flying saucers really exist think that there is no such thing.

4 Write a Three-Paragraph Summary

Answers vary.

Lesson 11

1 Use These Words in Sentences

Answers vary.

2 What Do You Think?

Answers vary.

3 Combine the Sentences

1. Allen is an unhappy, angry person who is lonely because other people stay away from him.
2. Sue has many friends because she is a happy person who impresses other people as being friendly and open.
3. Fran accepts herself and other people, so she doesn't often get upset or angry.

4 Write a Three-Paragraph Summary

Answers vary.

Lesson 12

1 Use These Words in Sentences

Answers vary.

2 What Do You Think?

Answers vary.

3 Combine the Sentences

1. Anne Frank was a young Jewish girl who lived in an attic with seven other people for more than two years.
2. Anne kept a diary she called "Kitty," which she started when she was thirteen and wrote in until she was fifteen. *or* When she was thirteen, Anne started a diary that she called "Kitty" and wrote in until she was fifteen.
3. On October 9, 1942, Anne had depressing news about her family's friends, who were loaded into cattle trucks and taken to a large Jewish camp.

4 Write a Three-Paragraph Summary

Answers vary.

Lesson 13

1 Use These Words in Sentences

Answers vary.

2 What Do You Think?

Answers vary.

3 Put These Sentences in Order

1. Hitler's army invaded Poland.
2. Hitler's war machine crushed five countries in three months.
3. Japan attacked Pearl Harbor, Hawaii.
4. The United States declared war on Japan and Germany.
5. Anne Frank died in one of Hitler's camps.
6. World War II ended.

4 Write Paragraphs

Answers vary.

Lesson 14

1 Use These Words in Sentences

Answers vary.

2 What Do You Think?

Answers vary.

3 Combine the Sentences

1. The camel is a desert animal that can carry people and cargo hundreds of miles with little food or water.
2. The United States tried using camels in the 1850's when the army brought camels from Africa and Asia to carry cargo from Texas to California.
3. The camel has a hump that can weigh eighty pounds or more and is used to store fat, not water.

4 Write Paragraphs

Answers vary.

Lesson 15

1 Use These Words in Sentences

Answers vary.

2 What Do You Think?

Answers vary.

3 Put These Sentences in Order

1. People who lived in the Stone Age were right-handed.
2. In 1903, a man in Italy said jails were filled with left-handed people.
3. Until the 1930's, children were forced to write with their right hands.
4. Any child who wrote with his left hand was slapped on the hand.
5. The classroom atmosphere is more peaceful now.
6. People still don't know much about this subject.

4 Write Paragraphs

Answers vary.

Lesson 16

1 Use These Words in Sentences

Answers vary.

2 What Do You Think?

Answers vary.

BOOK 4

3 Combine the Sentences

1. In libraries and bookstores, there are many books about dying, some packed with details, and some with step-by-step lessons for dying.
2. A French writer had a riding accident in which he was so badly hurt that his friends believed he was dead.
3. Pain is useful but it is likely to be turned off when there is no way back, which is the best way for it to be.

4 Write Paragraphs
Answers vary.

Lesson 17

1 Use These Words in Sentences
Answers vary.

2 What Do You Think?
Answers vary.

3 Put These Sentences in Order

1. James B. Brady was born in 1856.
2. Brady was first hired as a bellhop.
3. He became a successful salesman.
4. He was taken to the hospital.
5. Doctors learned that Brady's stomach was six times as large as normal.
6. Diamond Jim died in 1917.

4 Write Paragraphs
Answers vary.

Lesson 18

1 Use These Words in Sentences
Answers vary.

2 What Do You Think?
Answers vary.

3 Combine the Sentences

1. Life was hard in Ireland in the 1800's when people depended on the potato for their main food.
2. People only needed a spade to grow potatoes, but the potato was a dangerous crop because it did not keep and couldn't be stored until the next season.
3. More than a million people fled Ireland and went to America and England.

4 Write Paragraphs
Answers vary.

Lesson 19

1 Use These Words in Sentences
Answers vary.

2 What Do You Think?
Answers vary.

3 Put These Sentences in Order

1. The teeth break up food we eat.
2. Glands in the mouth release saliva.
3. The food is swallowed.
4. The stomach receives the food.
5. The food is churned by muscles in the stomach.
6. Digestion is completed in the small intestine.

4 Write Paragraphs
Answers vary.

Lesson 20

1 Use These Words in Sentences
Answers vary.

2 What Do You Think?
Answers vary.

3 Combine the Sentences

1. A little old lady looked up and saw a stranger who had ragged clothes but wore them without shame.
2. The stranger put the washtub on the fire and then went to the well, got some water, and put it in the washtub.
3. The young man was busy making soup, adding beans and tomatoes, but Granny did not see him do that. *or* The young man was busy adding beans and tomatoes to the soup, but Granny didn't see him do that.

4 Write Paragraphs
Answers vary.

Review

1 What Do You Think?
Answers vary.

2 Write Paragraphs
Answers vary.

3 Write a Three-Paragraph Story
Answers vary.

4 Write a Three-Paragraph Story
Answers vary.

BOOK 4